A Rain Ancestral

A Rain Ancestral

poems

Harold Whit Williams

San Antonio Review Press
Austin

Copyright. 2022. Harold Whit Williams. All rights reserved.

The author's moral rights have been asserted.

Library of Congress Cataloging-in-Publication Data
Names: Williams, Harold Whit. | Williams, Harold Whit, 10/11/1968–. A Rain Ancestral.
Title: A Rain Ancestral
Description: Paperback edition. | Austin: San Antonio Review Press/William O. Pate II, 2022.
Identifiers: LCCN 2022938233 | ISBN 9781736177983 (softcover)

Library of Congress Control Number: 2022938233
Record available at https://lccn.loc.gov/2022938233.

Published by
San Antonio Review Press/William O. Pate II
an imprint of *San Antonio Review*
2028 E. Ben White Boulevard #240-5735
Austin, Texas 78741
United States of America

Cover art by Ashley Savage Williams.

The first collection of poetry published by *San Antonio Review* Press, Austin, Texas, USA.

The publisher's father, William O. Pate, has converted former family farmland in southwest Alabama into new growth forest and enrolled it in the U.S. Department of Agriculture's Conservation Reserve Program in support of climate-change mitigation, covering at least a portion of the renewable resources required to produce print editions of this book.

Always read free at sareview.org

For Ashley, of course

Swallows are convening in the hollows
To keep me company for the final mile.
They swoop and twitter about a small rain
Coming, or somebody sure as the rain.

Gibbons Ruark

Contents

Acknowledgements   xi

Rest Measure

Silent Witness	3
Recently Unearthed Ambiguous Folktale	4
Give Me That Old Time Religion	5
Meta Love Story	6
Monster Movie	7
Manifest Destiny (Slight Return)	8
Magnetic North Still Life	9
Epiphany on the #10 Bus	10
No Hands Clapping	11
Binge-Watching The Detective	12
Dogdazed Nero	13
Blood Brothers Revisited	14
Rest Measure	15

A Rain Ancestral

The Old Country	19
To Andy at the Crown Liquor Saloon, Belfast	20
Troubles Outside the Duke of York, Belfast	21
To Tim in No Man's Land, Belfast	22
McHugh's in Belfast, Founded 1711	23
To the Toy Shop Owner in Newcastle	24
Mother's Day, County Down, Northern Ireland	25

To Julie at Quinn's Dreaming of España	26
To Pat Behind His Desk at the Donard Hotel	27
To Rob Rooney, the Merchant Marine Jesus of Newcastle, County Down	28
To that Odd Fellow Bellowing in the Dundrum Bus Station	29
Leaving County Down	30
To P.J. Murphy at Sweny's Chemist	31
To the Barman at O'Donoghue's: All Elbows & Scowl	32
Hallway Divertimento in F Major	33
To Larry Ducey Driving In His Weather	34
Bloomsday Unobserved	35

State Worker's Crown of Thorns

State Worker's Skeptical Bedtime Prayer	39
State Worker Swears Off Local News	40
State Worker Walks On Water, Then Complains That No One Saw Him	41
State Worker Considers the Concept of Dualism, Then Shrugs It Off as Metaphysical Smoke and Mirrors	42
State Worker Out-of-Tune With the Quotidian	43
State Worker Watches the Clock	44
State Worker Buried Alive in the Himalayas Of His Mind	45
State Worker Catches Himself in a Lie, Then Realizes Truth is Far More Interesting	46
State Worker Ponders His Life, Which Turns Out Is Just a Facsimile and Not Legally Binding	47
State Worker Out Upon His Walkabout Spies LBJ's Visage in the Old Campus Turtle Pond	48
State Worker Contemplates Time Travel After Spotting His Doppelganger in the Bathroom Mirror	49
State Worker Files Himself Away to Forget That Any of This Ever Happened	50

Apocalypse Cobwebs

Leaf Raking Afternoon Koan	53
Palm Sunday Phone Call	54
Death Eating a Cracker	55
Made For TV	56
A Black and White Movie	57
Apocalypse Cobwebs	58
Sad Ballad of Elsewhere	59
Lepisma Saccharina	60
Buried Alive On the Old Chisholm Trail	61
How The West Was Won	62
Psalm For Just Getting By	63
Wednesday Night Prayer Meeting	64
The After Afterlife	65
About the Author	67
Other Works by Harold Whit Williams	68
About San Antonio Review Press	69
Also Available from San Antonio Review Press	70

Acknowledgements

Some of these poems have been published in *The Cape Rock*, *Concho River Review*, *Kestrel*, *The Midwest Quarterly*, and *San Antonio Review*, to whose editors grateful acknowledgment is given.

REST MEASURE

Silent Witness

As nightfall came, all the shadows
Stitched themselves together
Into one immense funereal shroud.

Birds became skeletons
Displayed upon bare branches.
Daydreams spun in their little graves.

The TV and the radio
Stopped working,
For which I was grateful. And

One street over,
Either a car backfired
Or someone was shot to death.

I said nothing to no one,
Figuring that sooner or later
My time would come.

Recently Unearthed Ambiguous Folktale

Cloud cover for a change, but stretched thin
With soft flecks of blue showing.
Enough blue
To knit the cat a sweater,
Some grandmother might say, usually
When knitting.

Knitting a blanket blue and white or a quilt
For some young boy. The boy young
And selfish, haughty with others. The boy young
In body, old in spirit, eventually
Reversed to catastrophic effect.

But let us not dwell in the future.
Sharp green of the grandmother's loblolly pine.
Blue and white quilt of the young boy's sky.
He's halfway
Up the tree, grumbling, griping. Deaf
To those shrill calls for supper.

Dumb hands sap-sticky,
Grasping for more blue and white.
Blind to most everything beneath him.
He never makes it to the top, or back down,
In case you were wondering.

Give Me That Old Time Religion

Soft rain upon my lunchtime courtyard,
Upon my elm tree
With starlings,
Upon my jagged aura, my slicked-back hair.
Rain obfuscating future, soaking
Present to its bones,

Washing away the past in quick rivulets
Down root-cracked sidewalks.
Three days now, this rain.
Practically a new deity to worship,
To speak in tongues and chant to. I'm scribing

Commandments, proverbs,
Epistles and such in my
Lunchtime notebook, my
Drenched and inkblotted notebook.
Hosannas to rain!
For we shall tuck in to our little cloudbeds

And nightdream
The lightning flash, the thunder rumble.
We shall awaken
In our watery bodies, refreshed
And flowing forth from the source.

Meta Love Story

On the way to the grave I met a woman.
A real catch, they all said.
Legs of a showgirl, hands of a rancher.
Heart like a stone
At the bottom of the sea.
She built us a home
Out on the cold hard prairie.
She tucked me in at night like the child
We never had.
I wrote her ballads – evenings, weekends –
And disappeared slowly
As was my nature.
She brightened like a star to engulf
The both of us.
We're happier now.
We burn in darkness.

Monster Movie

Through the cracked curtain of morning
A creature is seen.
It is slinking down the frontage road.
It is dripping with daylight.

Howling invectives
To each and every commuter,
It rises up on hind legs
To daze us all with its shiny underside.

I stay put with my books, with my
Albums and pictures.
I put the kettle on and cover all clock faces.
I turn my gaze inward

And leave the middle path to others.
Time's rampage
Rages elsewhere, but this purgatory
Is mine and mine alone.

Manifest Destiny (Slight Return)

We had a good run, I do declare.
The pomp and circumstantial evidence.
The bomb's earthly delight.

All you can eat. No down-payments.
Bottomless refills. Crotchless panties.
Low fat. No credit. This will

Make your toes curl in pleasure.
Add length and girth.
Fuck you, fantasy football.

Shithole country music. Live free
Or diet. That Blue Angels
Flyover cured my Covid.

Magnetic North Still Life

Sparrows of course, and low morning clouds
Off the Gulf. Always

Some heft to the air. I am always
Waking so far to the west.

Always working these here fingerbones,
Working them overtime, digging them

Into that hard clay
Of the past.

That past back east of the mind.
That future

A line of thunderstorms to the south.
That present

A nagging passenger pointing me
Into the right direction.

Enough out of you, backseat driver,
There is no such place as home.

Epiphany on the #10 Bus

Dreamlost in this moment beneath a sky
Saharan and summer-struck,
Beneath heat/hate shimmerings,

Beneath a heaven stripped of meaning.
But an OK day spent
Down here in the land of plenty.

Papers pushed. Keys punched.
Our once cubicle-sized souls shrinking
To the size of Swingline staplers.

Soon enough, I'll store mine
In an empty Altoids tin. I'll rattle it
As I'm waiting for the 3:15 uptown.

I'll bury it in the backyard
Beside those basement tapes,
Those bunting bones. What's left of me

Minty-fresh inside a little metal box.
A resting place befitting no one.
A time capsule filled with nothing.

No Hands Clapping

Almost dark of a false dawn light.
Dry gust of west wind.
Sundried redbud leaves spin
And clatter down
Like a peasant child's toys.

Last night's whiskey still mixing it up
At the cellular level.
No breakthrough in my meditation.
No lesson learned
Living to see another sunrise.

I'm ramping down on cause/effect.
I'm gearing up
For all that future nothingness.
Spin and clatter, grasshopper,
Spin and clatter on the short way down.

Binge-Watching The Detective

The Lord of Darkness shuffles up and down the hall.
He rattles his hell-chains,

He keens and moans his graveyard blues.
Keep it down, I yell.

This is the final episode of Icelandic Murders,
Goddamnit.

After awhile, he draws up a chair
And drifts down into it.

That's more like it, I say, sliding him
The popcorn bowl.

We all sit back, giving in to inertia.
The glow off the flat screen

Illuminates our faces like morning sunshine,
Leaving nothing to the imagination.

Dogdazed Nero

Burnt end of August. Charred. Smoked.
Each desiccated day
Memory-foamed from the previous.
The streets and rooftops a heat mirage.
The metal silence of a city
Lulled to sleep.
I'm on the back steps, casting about
For a piece of the transcendent.
I'm banishing stray thoughts
To the edges of self.
Another cup of coffee.
Another messy meditation.
The whole world seemingly on fire
While I fiddle with the remote
And watch it burn.

Blood Brothers Revisited

A coworker says *blackberries* and I'm ten again
In that bramble beside the pasture.
Tom is barefoot and giggling.
Our lips purple from the ripe fruit.
I carry daddy's binoculars
And his sense of impending doom
Around my sunburned neck.
Mosquito hum. Meadowlark mantra.
Far-off rumble of the Memphis train.
Our sticky fingers. Our aching bellies.
That sky a blueline map of forever.
Tom pulls a pocketknife to swear an oath
For all gods listening or not.
He slices our palms and we touch
For the transfusion. We touch
To mingle meanings. We touch, then let go.
Decades have passed, that pasture
Now a neighborhood,
Yet I can still taste the tartness
Of a childhood Saturday. I can still hear
Those meadowlarks, the mosquito hum.
I can still see the scar,
And feel that faintest pulse
Of a dear friend's summer heartbeat.

Rest Measure

A ringing in the ears on the Ides of March.
A quivering of the spirit,
A glissando of sorts.
Some humming of that tuning fork
In the center of the soul.

And through an open window wafts
The major-thirds of a dove's coo,
Then silence. Such the silence.
The silence of grandmother's voice,
Of mother's voice.

The silence of sleet melting
On a sun-warmed street.
The engine killed. The wind dying down.
Far-off thunder
Awakened from its daydream.

That last chord struck
On the old parlor piano, years ago,
Still dissolving
Into the dust-shrouded air.
D minor. The saddest of all keys.

A RAIN ANCESTRAL

The Old Country

There on the map but vague in my mind.
Blurred through the window
As we touch down in rain.

Rain like some shroud to be lifted.
A rain ancestral
And singing of pity.

This is the dream that will happen.
This is how it will all play out.
There will be seagulls

And pints of stout and my face
Around every corner.
There will be you in the air

And you on the ground.
There will be us in our cups
At the end of the bar. Sad ballads

To drink in the lingering light.
Welcome home, perfect strangers.
Welcome the heaven of peace.

To Andy at the Crown Liquor Saloon, Belfast

Ornate these windows stained – a sinner's cathedral
For quiet, lasting peace. Across the street
That oft-bombed station sits, but here you pull
Our first abroad refreshments. Pints of stout
And whiskeys neat. Correct response, you say
To ice or water. Not lagged by jet just yet,
We cheers and quaff. We marvel at the way
Our lives have brought us here, amazed, in debt
To you, kind sir. I'd like to pass away
Inside this bar old Betjeman preserved!
The Protestant hooch, the Catholic stout, my belly
Not troubled, just ceasing fire and full. I'm led
To love this place: no television, no music.
Your hands upon the taps a magician's trick.

Troubles Outside the Duke of York, Belfast

Down an alley with the sun behind clouds
We stagger like payday Protestants,
We gripe like backpew Catholics.
That fiddle tune in my head.
That Target ad in yours.

Northern whiskey and southern stout
Bickering in our bloodstreams.
The blood boiling with love. With hate.
The blood tempered
By time and its unlikely loyalties.

We will fight without honor.
We will surrender with indignity.
Christ upon the cross!
How many goddamned times
Can the other cheek be turned?

To Tim in No Man's Land, Belfast

Surprised to hear your brogue requesting bourbon,
We turn with eyebrows raised. I cannot take
That boggy water of life, you laugh. My kin
Will never know. But friends beside you poke
And take the piss to diss all night. You're smacked
That Yanks would ride a bus up here. No strife
For now, you sigh, but picture sidewalks flecked
With blood, with brains, and snipers on the roof.
We sip our silence, reverent travelers. Your home
Is gapped between those troubled Ulster tribes.
You slur Kentucky in your throat. So time,
It heals, but schools still segregate. And bombs
Are made in other places, but children grow
To hate the Other. We pay our tab, then go.

McHugh's in Belfast, Founded 1711

We pour ourselves into a back booth
As the trad music begins.
My ragged breath
Inflates the bagpiper's ego.
My glass had whiskey. Now it doesn't.

The afternoon passes like a gypsy's cart
As that fiddler reels
Some peat bog melody. Something
From the mists and the rocks
And the heather,

Something from the Scots soaked
In stag's blood and milk.
I will die for this song.
In a field beside the sea I will die
For this very song.

My bones hollowed-out and whistling
In the wind. A dirge for the days
I can no longer remember.
No spirits, just smoke.
Just smoke in the heaven of sky.

To the Toy Shop Owner in Newcastle

Our day turns bright and brisk – the Irish Sea
A waking dream. Into your store we pop
For trinkets, baubles, a niece's gift. To be
Or not to be? I'd surely like to stop
With questions existential here amongst
These dolls and bears and such. The owner notes
My tipsy drawl, inquires about the angst
Back home. Its time and temp. Those reckless votes
For a feckless TV lout. We groan, then switch
The subject: weather, whiskey. She rings us up
And speaks of Dallas, Vegas, American kitsch,
A visit with her husband. We'll gladly swap
With you, I quip. That misty view beyond
Your window magick. Worth every pound.

Mother's Day, County Down, Northern Ireland

We empty our pockets of quid at Quinn's
And take our full bladders down to the promenade.
Magpies and jackdaws laughing.
Kelp the color of my younger man's beard.
A small rain gathering atop the high peaks

And Slieve Donard flexes above us
Like a crofter's hard bicep. Mourne Mountains
Sweeping down to such a sweet surf, as you
Point out sheep and seagulls along Main Street.
I mourn this holiday as is my old country custom –

Grieve and drink. Grieve and drink.
I weep and gnash my National Health teeth.
Let us turn our backs on the village of Yesterday.
Let us sing along with Mother Water.
Hear her murmuring in each crashing wave?

To Julie at Quinn's Dreaming of España

You have your own Gibraltar south of town
It seems – the Donard in its clouds and mist.
On clearing afternoons atop the cairn
A soul can spy the Isle of Man. You'd best
Uncork that tempranillo by the Bass
And tonic water, pour a glass and grind
Your heels flamenco style. O ginger lass!
This world is small and travel's in the mind.
Just find a sunny spot with wine and song,
With lover's hands and lips. My body aches
From sleepless nights, from airport lines so long
And tiny seatings. For blessed Jesus' sake,
Madrid will always be there when you're able
And ready. Another round, please, for the table.

To Pat Behind His Desk at the Donard Hotel

And here's that mizzly weather you predicted
Just yesterday. The Mournes are crowned with clouds
Of Nordic nature. Mizzly, you grinned then said –
A mist and drizzle mixed. Those Irish moods
That we had hoped for: gray and low. McGinn's,
You roar, will pour the proper pint next door.
The best in town, turns out. We bird the Glenn
And thereabouts for thrushes, gulls, and more,
But thirst sets in, and soon. Those stouts go down
Like mother's milk and just as nourishing.
Upon return, we fill you in. That clown
We'd left behind comes up – bada-bing
This orange nightmare presidential mishap.
You misquote Chomsky, then tip your woolen cap.

To Rob Rooney, the Merchant Marine Jesus of Newcastle, County Down

You let us sit and sip awhile and soak
The local colors in. They're gray like soot
And green from what I've seen so far. You croak
Hello and pull from us our Texas roots
With ease and gentle guile. Don't call me sir,
You quip, then laugh, a smile within that wizard's
Unkempt beard. Authority's a cur
To kick repeatedly to the curb, so towards
Our drinks we turn, the wife and I. You buy
A round, and buy another. We speak of rock
And roll and pipe and fiddle tunes, as whiskey
Imbibed lets loose our traveler's tongues. Your shtick
Is staying put from all those years at sea.
Don't ever sell your home, you say and sigh.

To that Odd Fellow Bellowing in the Dundrum Bus Station

Someday I'll sip your share of grief, my friend
And fellow traveler. Your tattered sweater and smoke-
From-burning-peat discolored hair. You bend
Those clichéd Paddy rules – a jacket Nike-
Emblazoned, charity shop-acquired, I'm sure.
The wife and I gaze down to let you pray
Your moans in privacy. Others stare:
Amused, disgusted. Begging's not your way
It seems, just whiskey weeping. Stout atonement.
I'm just about to cry for drink myself,
But here's our bus to Newry. You sit and slant
Across the aisle for several miles as if
The world has tilted, then pull the cord to stop
In nowhere's middle. *Sláinte*, sod and sheep!

Leaving County Down

From the Newcastle bus we spy Savage's Pub
In the Castlewellan square,
Exactly where that fellow in McKen's
Said it would be.
He had pulled our pints the night before
And peered into your past.
His granny a Savage from thereabouts.
His voice a drunken piper's drone.
He rubbed stubble
On what could've been your father's face
And spoke of many more about.
Savages. Ulster crofters
With France in their veins.
Our stouts settled.
The air in the room settled.
Liverpool vs. Somebody
On a muted corner telly. Your mother a Stout
And your father a Savage, and now
I'm holding your hand
On this day bus to Dublin. So many names.
So many names stacked
Like gray stones in the fallow fields.
And those green hills rising up,
Daring us to believe in them.

To P.J. Murphy at Sweny's Chemist

A shop the size of Joyce's piney box
That's cool and quiet to boot. Your darting eyes
The gray of gulls. Moher. Your longish locks
A necromancer's white. I've crossed the seas
To seize that fabled lemon soap, to tune
A folk guitar and hear you strum, caress
That ballad from *The Dead*. Of Dublin town,
Encyclopedic knowledge you possess:
The previous names of pubs and such. I grab
A book or two, then strain to follow suit
Our conversation. This southern gift of gab –
Your Cork, my Alabama – plays on and out
Until I ask about your namesake stout.
Try Mary's Bar, you grin, off Grafton Street.

To the Barman at O'Donoghue's: All Elbows & Scowl

We take our seats and order stout and wait
For music trad to weep to. A corner perch
To nurse our pints. They're late, the twats – you spit,
Then glare at tourists soaking in the kitsch
And blarney shite to sell. The other server,
He gives you lee and sideways glances. I'm drunk
Enough to laugh behind your back, you punter
Befouled with sweat and piss. Your frame a tank
That's panzered down a lout or two, I'll bet.
Another round you bring, then frown to spy
My coins as tip upon the bar. A set
Begins: the banjo pluck, the fiddle cry.
I ask to buy your drink, which shows my hand
And makes you smirk – Oh, the gentleman!

Hallway Divertimento in F Major

Hotel Mont Clare, Dublin, Ireland

On my hung-over way to the corner chemist
For your NSAIDs and ointments,
For my antacid tablets and Band-Aids,
I find myself paused – in awe –
Outside our next-door neighbors' room.
Their afternoon duet has drawn me in
With its rudimentary rhythms,
With its haunting, high-pitched
Biological imperative. Upon each *uhh* and *aah*
I blink like some smalltown Baptist
Beholding midnight French cinema.
No DO NOT DISTURB sign dangling,
No housekeeping staff in sight,
So I take one step closer
And imagine my musical role within a trio.
O those little youthful deaths to mourn!
O bittersweet autumn of the bones!
The back goes. The sap slows. And you
In our room having a headache lie-down.
Tempo quickening, pitches rising,
But before the performance can climax
I shuffle off towards the elevator.
And later, after dinner, the two of us
Will sit up in bed holding hands,
Falling asleep to some old movie:
The car chase, the fireworks,
The bullet train penetrating its tunnel.

To Larry Ducey Driving In His Weather

Our final Irish morning lowered temps
And somberly rained. Those days and days of sun
Had dazzled pasty locals. They'd shed their tops
And basked like gila monsters spread upon
The desert floor. But now, our luggage stuffed
And in your taxi's trunk – Old Dirty Dublin,
Goodbye, we say! Adieu to Sweny's: closed.
Adios to Davy Byrne's: closed. The M-1
Is sparse this early, and heading north, you speak
Of recent snows and mizzle. You've come to love
That low and graying gloom. Your inner clock
Is winding down, you say, so stop and lave
It all of doom and rest beside your fire
With tea and smokes. O blessed, sodden Eire.

Bloomsday Unobserved

The trouble with a mask is that
Sometimes it won't come off.

Go with it – says my sensei.
Assume the position –
Says that clock beside my bed.

There is always a seat at the bar
For the thirsty, for the incognito.

I am not a doctor
Nor do I play one on TV.
I have no grand literary allusion

For my delusions of grandeur.
No Cyclops metaphor here.

No smutty soliloquy. Just my
Everyday face worn & torn. Just
My useless yes I said yes I will Yes

STATE WORKER'S CROWN OF THORNS

State Worker's Skeptical Bedtime Prayer

O Lord, methinks I'll call you Lord. Are you
Affixed up there on high, or somewhere else?
And us lowdown in murk mistaking blue
Above as heaven, hell beneath cool grass.

It matters not to me, as I assume
Some gods cannot exist except in dreams,
In trifling songs. I guess most folks presume
To hear from you by way of simple hymns

Or over-the-counter meds hallucinations.
My mood's been altered by rum. I'd like to mellow
And spy just once, you, big fellow. Creations
Upon creations! So, might I feast on crow?

This bottle's full of nothing. I'll say good night
And find the faith to know you'll get the lights.

State Worker Swears Off Local News

My morning ramble crosses a creek, the place
They found that murdered girl. O Lord, we need
Some answers right away. Behind each face –
Just ruthless animal urge? A dark, indeed,

An evil core to all? I'm tired, so tired
Of talking to myself instead of you,
Which turns out is the same. How weird
Yet natural our synapses flaring blue

In prayer, in dreams, in blinding rage or love.
But where were you, almighty? If everywhere
As some do say, confess to this and save
Us all our grief. Let's strip your altar bare

Of monster-fingered idols. In fits and starts
We'll keep such things to ponder in our hearts.

State Worker Walks On Water, Then Complains That No One Saw Him

For lunch I'm thinking noodles, soup, Korean –
Bulgogi, Katsu chicken. Might even sneak
A glass of wine or three. And all I've seen
So far today will sink into this creek

To bloat and rot. Already doubling down
The ones, the zeros. Show these campus twats
Just how it's done! I'm out here on my own
Without a float, a vest for life. It's

Almost time to rock this air-guitar
For real, to hammer-on and pick-squeal.
Extended-jam this second coming. A star
Is born alright, then burns and flares a spell

Before it cools to disappear. These kids
Today! Their gadgets! Oblivious on meds...

State Worker Considers the Concept of Dualism, Then Shrugs It Off as Metaphysical Smoke and Mirrors

Again with lightning bugs and blooms. The grass
A resurrected green that dusk deepens,
Enhances even. Blinking, blinking no less
Realistic as mushroom trips, sci-fi zines.

The bedroom window cracked, my lover's breath
Upon my throat, and Coltrane keening, shrieking
From down the hall. It's either this or death?
A heaven. Hell. Am I to lay here begging

Forgiveness of sins? And just what sins are those
But ones of survival? Nature; nurture. Science
Is on my side for sure, but cannot close
The deal, blast one past the outfield fence.

So thanks, I guess, for nothing. Maybe thanks
For separating thoughts from what one thinks.

State Worker Out-of-Tune With the Quotidian

O heaven's album spinning backwards! O Lord
Of hosts and highway diner hostesses!
It seems I cannot live the life of bard.
Although, sometimes I let a song possess

My feeble mind. I sing it in the shower.
I grow my hair and live the lyrics. I've played
To rooms just full of air-conditioned air
And noise and really nothing else. I've prayed

To sky just full of sky, etcetera…
But now I pluck the six-strings after work
To disappear inside a plethora
Of notes and chords. No smoke, no fire, no spark.

Today is just another ballad's verse,
Some bridge, some modulation to rehearse.

State Worker Watches the Clock

What say ye, Lord, to this timely topic of time?
I know those holy books we wrote are filled
With parables, koans apropos. No godly tome
Have I been able to grasp, however. So, could

We break it down between each other? They say
It crawls, it flies, it heals; it's even stopped
According to specific keepers. No way
It's ever stopped for me – quickened, slowed

For sure. But quantifying nature's doings
Seems ludicrous at best. Those little digits
Upon our wrists that measure moments. Comings
And goings X's off a calendar. What is it

With leaves that bud and green, then fall to fodder?
We sure as hell aren't getting any younger.

State Worker Buried Alive in the Himalayas Of His Mind

In movies, some brandy-bearing St. Bernard
Discovers snowbound hikers, drags them back
To Sherpa safety. This is not John Ford
However. Closer to John Waters. I lack

Internal fortitude, the will to do-or-die,
The heave and ho that's needed for this trek.
Extremities numb from paperwork...I say
A drink's in order. Goddamn that office clock!

Just dig me out and snap my pic for *Time*,
For *Life* and *National Geographic*. I'll scowl,
I'll frown Neanderthal-like if that will move
Some print. O how I missed my cubicle

And stapler! Pens and pencils, coffee mugs
And desk. Recycle, please, those travelogues.

State Worker Catches Himself in a Lie, Then Realizes Truth is Far More Interesting

It seems I've always been the praying sort,
If prayer is weeping along with FM songs
Upon the lonely road. That human heart
Will break in slow 4/4; the rights, the wrongs

Of childish lyrics; mélange of minor chords.
And all those setting suns I've spoken to
Intoning grace. Amen. Muttered words
That disappeared like smoke into the blue.

And birds, blossoms, breaking waves don't know
They're holy, perfect relics of a heaven
Existing only here, only now.
Just thank that winter moon, that summer sun.

Just thank those family photos on the shelf.
Just thank the stuff of stars you call yourself.

State Worker Ponders His Life, Which Turns Out Is Just a Facsimile and Not Legally Binding

This weather's odd for early May. A sky
As gray, autumnal-like as Hallow's Eve
With chilling wind for budded leaves. Don't try
To cipher meanings, plot and graph the jive

Of boundary demarcations. All talk is small
It seems, inconsequential, belittled
Before this vast creation. Sometimes I feel
Like Christ upon his cross: expired, naked,

And right about most everything. Methinks
I'll clamber off this Calvary for bagels
And breakroom coffee, and later, liquor drinks
To toast our pitchfork-wielding angels.

Who cares that time does not exist? Let's down
These whiskey replicas, then paint the town.

State Worker Out Upon His Walkabout Spies LBJ's Visage in the Old Campus Turtle Pond

Another day of rain. Those pigeons pious,
Conspiratorial, quiet. It comes a time
I'll huff around these forty acres – righteous
Employee gifted far beyond the tome

And cartographic realms. A seer! They've said.
Just take a water body, any size,
To telegraph for me a message. Dead,
Alive, it matters not the sender. Ablaze

His eyes, El Presidente thirty-six,
Ablaze with class resentment, booze and doom.
His hair grown long towards the end, he'd fix
A glass of tea to watch the flowers bloom

Along the Pedernales. Saving face,
He said, is just a way to lose your ass.

State Worker Contemplates Time Travel After Spotting His Doppelganger in the Bathroom Mirror

Returned from future haunts, myself, to warn
Myself of past mistakes to come – the fuck?
And seems I've held up well, it's good to learn,
With hair still there, some space-age nip and tuck.

But vocal sounds did not transmute the trip
Dimension-wise. And reading lips? I can't.
At least myself today. Is this a trap
We all get snared in? Peeved, recalcitrant,

My future-me has grown (and that I could
Predict, at least), gesticulating now
So wildly up towards a patch of mould.
Apparently, our high-falutin' know-and-how

Gets bested up against The Allergens.
I long to ask myself about my fins…

State Worker Files Himself Away to Forget That Any of This Ever Happened

Such peace. Such boundless peace down here between
Out-dated forms, reports. That soothing hum
Of after-hours vacuum cleaners. I'm in
Like Flynn, gone triplicate with sheets-of-time,

Evaluations, memorandums. Then – quiet.
An afterlife of sorts. No messages,
No calls from friend or foe or kin, albeit
Was never one to stay in touch. Who rages

Against these dying lights? I shut them off
A long-ish time ago. Such boundless peace
In hanging folders hung. I used to scoff
At documents, the ticker-taping vice

Of clerks, etcetera. But maybe heaven
Exists in cabinet-form. I'm paper-thin!

APOCALYPSE COBWEBS

Leaf Raking Afternoon Koan

I find myself ankle-deep in red oak leaves.
Little drops of blood.
Little drops of bye-bye now.
Mother's sky is overarching in Glory,
Always expanding,
Blue and vast in its blurred beyondness.
Mine is shrinking, shrouding
Head and shoulders
Like the shawl of some smoking peasant.
I sweater-fold my sky
At the dusky dark end of a workday
To place on the shelf
With all other sundries. I drift off
Into wine-sleep.
I snore my prayers and awaken godless.
Mother sings to her sky.
The very memory of her voice
Shakes the grass blades above her.
Who am I to question memory or voice?
Sky or oak leaves?
Caught between tomorrow and yesterday
I am, wrapped
In a shawl of sky, smoking,
Shuffling through the blood-red drops,
Becoming a memory of myself.

Palm Sunday Phone Call

That tired Lenten voice of my faraway father
On the other end of the line,
Weather-beaten and weak,
Faint but full of forgiveness. His voice

Is an almost holy relic
In its ninth decade. His voice
Riding into the village on an ass
Under the scrutinous centurion eyes

Of the past. A crowd gathers round,
Disembodied and bodied. I hear them
Beeping in on the other line.
They are colleagues and family,

They are students and loved ones.
They reach out to touch the hem of his garment.
They weep and they gnash their teeth.
And I am by the side

Of his long and meandering pathway,
Waving those green fronds
Of pride and of envy. I, who have led
The peasant's life of a hapless onlooker.

I, who will leave nothing behind
But a thin shroud of what-ifs.
The stone not rolled away.
Nothing much to be saved.

Death Eating a Cracker

A bird sick of its tree, I despair.
−Frank Stanford

Along the muddy river banks, lost
In brambled memories,
Those rags and bags of stray thoughts
Caught high
In floodmarked branches.
The mind wanders, of course.
The mind some wayfaring stranger.
An orphan in sackcloth
Singing old ballads for a nickel.
The very idea of negation,
Of loss, coal-smudged upon
The mind's face.
The mind buck dances and hollers.
The mind draws blood
Without wincing. The mind traps
Rabbits in that field behind the barn.
A shadow overtakes the mind,
A shadow with no name
And cast by nothing.
The water rises, then falls. The mind
Called home at last.
All is right with the world.

Made For TV

I stand tall in the prairie grass,
Final scene of a movie never made.
Smoke signals. Wildfires

On the horizon.
A dove coos one last time.
Lonesome dove.

Last of the Mohicans.
I squat in a clearing, chewing
Mescal beans

To envision all those gods
I created. I hum
The closing credit's theme.

I lie down
In the shadow my life cast.
I would like to thank the academy.

A Black and White Movie

For Boris Grebenschchikov

Having stepped through the doorway
Into a dream of the Great War,
I call back to those ancestors
Who've hidden me in the closet of time.

The tiny streets are now silent.
Ashes settled on the toys and bones.
Clothes hung out to dry
On the long guns of stalled tanks.

Laws are meaningless, of course,
And they always have been.
The limp dictator
Hangs from a metal girder.

Come out, I call
To all those ghosts behind me.
Let the day have its way with us.
Come out and watch the credits roll.

Apocalypse Cobwebs

For Scott in Prague

Seems I've been stockpiling my time
All along. Hording daydreams
Like canned beans.
Watching reruns of past grievances
And misunderstandings.

But from beyond this dirty window
Those new leaves shine
With a clean green malevolence.
And from down the street
Comes the low moan of hungry buses.

Nothing left for it
But to don this mask that is my face,
Hunker down
Inside these brittle bones,
And wash my hands of it all.

Sad Ballad of Elsewhere

This is the dream we all sing dead of night.
Dead to the world
We all seem to be. Dead can dance.
Dead by August.
This is my call to prayer I snore in C.
This is the verse/chorus/bridge
Of that deep album track
I lost my virility to.
Joy is a blue note, random
And fleeting. Grief is a rhythm section
Always in the pocket.
With a frown we wake to rewrite
Each day's melody.
With a smile we're lowered
Into that rest measure beneath the sod.

Lepisma Saccharina

Mother would flip through the leafy folds
Of her old family Bible as silverfish
Swam up the spines with tiny legs
A Creator surely did not give them.

She would point her stubby finger
At the still living and the long dead.
She would click her tongue with bug sounds
And say – Would you just look at that.

She'd say – Lord he was a handsome thing.
She'd say – Mean as a snake that one.
She'd say – Hey boy, gimme some sugar.
But it was salt she poured

In an older man's wounds. Or any man's.
Neighbor. Pastor. Son-in-law.
Her husband gladly worked three jobs
Just to stay out of the house.

His skin grew as thick and hard
As exoskeleton. He lived on dewdrops
And the dried glue of days. In time,
He grew wings but never learned to fly.

Buried Alive On the Old Chisholm Trail

Something went wrong beside the dry creek.
A late winter sky reborn in its own image.
The neighbor's radio buzz, the four-lane drone,
Etcetera. Amen. I have my soul pressed up

Against the cracked living room window,
Seeking out that shaggy buffalo vibe.
I've made friends here in the temporal world.
I've heard ghosts down inside the stereo.

The past is not your friend, someone sang,
The future not your enemy. And my hair
And my fingernails of late have grown longer.
There's a tang of prairie upon my tongue.

How The West Was Won

During the day all those tiny houses
Shudder and sway. They whisper
To each other. They gossip. They lie.
Emptied, creaking, their occupants

Gone off to the endless war,
Gone off to the rat laboratories.
And the ground is of no use –
Cracking underneath foundations.

And the sky is of no use – clouds
Petroglyphing nothing in particular.
But it will be night soon enough.
All those tiny ghosts returning,

Their faces hung in parlor portraits.
Their breath filling up each room.
Their wet snores simple prayers
Seeking forgiveness, seeking peace.

Psalm For Just Getting By

For a few seconds there
The afternoon stopped breathing.

The afternoon flatlined
And we all kept walking past

Like Levite priests
On the road to Jericho.

Resuscitated by rain,
The afternoon grew around us.

And those little white moths
I've dreamt are everywhere now.

In the gray growing air.
In my speech. On this page's poem.

I didn't want to go there
But was led by a higher power.

Please don't look away, I pray.
Please don't look away.

Wednesday Night Prayer Meeting

Afternoon drone of the number 10 bus
Has me ten again as well
In a Methodist pew, hearing that epileptic
Fellow one row back
Monotoning *How Great Thou Art*.
And even at such an unadulterated age

I'm thinking *Maybe Not So Much*.
How senseless our beseeching seems
As my Buster Browns pinch,
As my stomach longs for loaves and fishes.
The very air around us
Unspectacular and unhaunted

By a holy ghost or any other spirit.
Forgive me Charles Mingus
And my mother in her grave. I tried
To get it in my soul.
I sought the Son and the Father
But found only rock and roll.

The After Afterlife

By the time you read this I will be gone.
Gone in the sense of not here.
Gone like a train
In the song of the same name.
Long gone, forgotten gone, the getting
Good and gone.

This is not a note left for loved ones.
This is not a cry for help,
Nor a shout into the abyss.
It's just that
Sundays can smother you with a pillow,

Roll up your corpse
Inside a Persian rug to drop
Into the metaphorical river. Gone
I said and I meant it.
Gone my cellular structure.
Reordered and replicated and processed

By someone else's hazel eyes.
Overheard down the hallway. Overlooked
In the morning mirror.
My shadow cast on that sidewalk bending
To the hard luck heaven of nowhere.

About the Author

Harold Whit Williams is a prize-winning poet and longtime guitarist for the critically acclaimed indie rock band Cotton Mather. A multiple Pushcart Prize nominee, he is recipient of the *Mississippi Review* Poetry Prize, the Robert Phillips Poetry Chapbook Prize, and the 2020 FutureCycle Press Poetry Book Prize. The author of six books of poetry and one short-story collection, Williams lives in Austin, Texas where he catalogs music for UT Austin and releases lo-fi jangle pop recordings as Daily Worker.

Other Works by Harold Whit Williams

Poetry:

- My Heavens
- Red Clay Journal
- Lost in the Telling
- Backmasking
- Waiting For The Fire To Go Out

Short fiction:

- Mel Bay's Book of the Dead

About San Antonio Review Press

A *Rain Ancestral* is the first single-author poetry collection published by *San Antonio Review*'s book publishing imprint, *San Antonio Review* Press.

San Antonio Review Press, an imprint of *San Antonio Review*, a nonprofit international literary, arts and ideas journal since 2017, is devoted to publishing book-length works by interesting voices.

Learn more at sareview.org/press.

San Antonio Review publishes original essays, poetry, art, reviews, theory and other work once a week on its website. Print issues are published at the publisher's discretion. Founded in San Antonio in 2017, SAR is based in Austin, Texas.

San Antonio Review is devoted to serving as a gathering space outside academia, the market and government for writers, artists, scholars, activists, workers, students, parents and others to express their perspectives and reflections on our shared world and help develop visions of our collective future. Funded by its publisher's income from his day jobs, donations and the sale of print editions and other materials and led and maintained by an all-volunteer editorial collective, SAR is not beholden to any institution, organization or ideology.

SAR is a seed.[1] Planted and tended, we hope it grows. We can at best provide a hospitable environment and some nurturing care to the pieces we publish and ensure their dissemination and preservation in hopes some future finder(s) may be spurred to positive action by what they share. The SAR Editorial Collective is an experiment[2] in the prefigurative politics of constructive, everyday resistance.[3] That is, SAR is trying to create a publishing organization today that reflects the world as it might be; that proves an alternative is possible and things may be otherwise.

Always read free at sareview.org

---

1. Credit for first likening SAR to a tree goes to our inaugural poetry editor Alex Z. Salinas in his introduction to our second print issue.
2. Süß, Rahel. "Horizontal Experimentalism: Rethinking Democratic Resistance." *Philosophy & Social Criticism*, Aug. 2021, https://doi.org/10.1177/01914537211033016.
3. Kristin Wiksell (2020) Worker cooperatives for social change: knowledge-making through constructive resistance within the capitalist market economy, *Journal of Political Power*, 13:2, 201-216, DOI: 10.1080/2158379X.2020.1764803

Also Available from San Antonio Review Press

Mel Bay's Book of the Dead
Stories by Harold Whit Williams

Six-string and stompbox-themed stories culled from a bittersweet and simpler South, a grotesque and good-riddance South. Think Youth Fiction peppered with HBO cussin'. Not necessarily for the faint-of-heart or the high-minded literati.

Print ISBN 9781736177921
Ebook ISBN 9781736177938
142 pages
January 15, 2021
San Antonio Review Press
https://doi.org/10.21428/9b43cd98.993e3fc9

City Lights From the Upside Down
Stories by Alex Z. Salinas

A rollercoaster in the middle of the Texas desert. (Or is it just a mirage?)

Print ISBN 9781736177976
Ebook ISBN 9781736177969
286 pages
September 3, 2021
San Antonio Review Press
https://doi.org/10.21428/9b43cd98.985162ab

Read excerpts at sareview.org/press.

www.ingramcontent.com/pod-product-compliance
Lightning Source LLC
Chambersburg PA
CBHW012007090526
44590CB00026B/3912